Guitar 1

INTRODUCTION

W9-BVH-016

You bought a guitar...so now what?

Congratulations! You look great holding that new guitar. But won't your friends and family be even more impressed if you can actually play the darn thing? In just a couple of weeks, we'll have you playing some cool riffs, as well as jamming on some full songs. By the end of this book, it's on to the hits—the Beatles, Clapton, Hendrix and many more—in the *FastTrack* songbooks.

All we ask is that you observe the three Ps: **patience**, **practice** and **pace yourself**.

Don't try to bite off more than you can chew, and DON'T skip ahead. If your fingers hurt, take the day off. If you get frustrated, put it down and come back later. If you forget something, go back and learn it again. If you're having a great time, keep on playing. Most importantly, have fun.

ABOUT THE AUDIO

*G*lad you noticed the bonus material—audio tracks! Each music example has been recorded so you can hear how it sounds and play along when you're ready. The examples are preceded by a one-measure count-off to indicate tempo and meter. Hal Leonard's **PLAYBACK+** allows you to emphasize the guitar part by panning right, or the accompaniment by panning left. This symbol will indicate an audio track is available for the example:

To access audio visit:
www.halleonard.com/mylibrary

Enter Code
6289-0116-6155-3084

ISBN 978-0-7935-7399-8

HAL•LEONARD®

7777 W. BLUEMOUND RD. P.O. BOX 13819 MILWAUKEE, WI 53213

Visit Hal Leonard Online at
www.halleonard.com

PARTS OF THE GUITAR
What a beauty!

Below are pictures of a standard electric guitar and a standard acoustic (steel-string) guitar. Get acquainted with the parts of your guitar, and, heck, give it a name if you want. You'll be spending a lot of time together.

head

tuning keys

nut

neck

frets

fingerboard

position markers

soundhole

body

pick guard

pickups

saddle

pickup selector switch

tone/volume controls

bridge

output jack

electric guitar

acoustic guitar

TUNING

When you tune, you correct the pitch of each string. **Pitch** means how high or low a musical tone is. This is adjusted by tightening (or loosening) the string, using the tuning keys on the head of the guitar. The tighter the string, the higher the pitch.

Your six guitar strings should be tuned to the pitches **E-A-D-G-B-E** (low to high).

CAUTION: Tighten slowly and not too much, or you'll be heading back to the store to buy new strings!

Piano tuning

No, you aren't about to tune an entire piano! If you have a piano or electric keyboard nearby, play the above notes one at a time and tune the corresponding guitar string until its pitch matches that of the piano.

Electric tuner

If you don't have the luxury of a piano or keyboard, you may want to purchase an electric guitar tuner.

A tuner will "listen" to each string as you play it and indicate whether the pitch is too high or too low.

Don't give up hope...if you don't have a piano and you can't buy a tuner, there's yet another solution:

Relative tuning

To tune your guitar by ear, you must tune the strings to each other. This is done in the following manner:

 Assuming string 6 is tuned correctly to E, press string 6 behind fret 5, play the depressed string 6 and open string 5 together. Adjust the pitch of string 5. When the two sounds match, you're in tune.

 Press string 5 behind fret 5 and tune open string 4 to it.

 Press string 4 behind fret 5 and tune open string 3 to it.

 Press string 3 behind fret 4 and tune open string 2 to it.

 Press the string 2 behind fret 5 and tune string 1 to it.

A FEW MORE THINGS
(...before we jam!)

Playing Positions

Perhaps the most comfortable and least tiring way to learn guitar is to sit while playing.

Once you learn a few tunes, feel free to stand up, but for now let's put that extra effort to better use—playing.

sitting

standing

Hold the neck of the guitar with your **left hand**, with the thumb resting comfortably behind the neck.

Hold the neck of the guitar slightly upwards—not downwards (at least not until you're on stage in front of thousands of fans and you're screaming through a solo).

Hold the pick in your **right hand** (when you're more advanced you can use your teeth, Jimi Hendrix-style).

left hand position (fingers)

left hand position (thumb)

right hand (with pick)

There's nothing stressful here, so don't grip the neck of your guitar too hard (you might strangle it!)

Strings & Frets

Fingerboard diagrams (or "grids") picture a portion of the fretboard and show you where to play the notes and chords. Circles with note names are drawn onto the diagram to indicate the notes played.

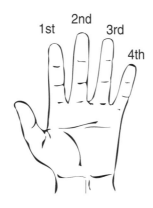

Think of your left-hand fingers as being numbered 1 through 4.

fold

DOG-EAR THESE TWO PAGES
(...you'll need to review them later)

Reading between the lines

Music is a language with its own symbols, structure, rules (and exceptions to those rules). To read, write, and play music requires knowing all the symbols and rules. But let's take it one step at a time (a few now, a few later)...

Notes

Music is written with symbols called **notes.** Notes come in all shapes and sizes. A note has two essential characteristics: its **pitch** (indicated by its position on the staff) and its **rhythmic value** (indicated by the following symbols):

𝅝	𝅗𝅥	𝅘𝅥
whole note	**half note**	**quarter note**

The rhythmic value lets you know how many beats the note lasts. Most commonly, a quarter note equals one beat. After that it's just like fractions:

two quarters equal a half

$$𝅘𝅥 + 𝅘𝅥 = 𝅗𝅥$$

two halves equal a whole

$$𝅗𝅥 + 𝅗𝅥 = 𝅝$$

four quarters equal a whole

$$𝅘𝅥\ 𝅘𝅥\ 𝅘𝅥\ 𝅘𝅥 = 𝅝$$

Staff

All the notes are positioned on (or nearby) a **staff,** which consists of five parallel lines and four spaces. (The plural for staff is "staves.") Each line and space represents a different pitch.

Leger Lines

Since not all notes will fit on just five lines and four spaces, **leger lines** (pronounced like "ledger") are used to extend the staff:

Clef

A symbol called a **clef** indicates which pitches appear on a particular staff. Music uses a variety of clefs, but we are only concerned with one for now:

Treble clef

A **treble clef** staff makes the lines and spaces have the following pitches:

An easy way to remember the line pitches is "**E**very **G**ood **B**and **D**raws **F**ans." For the spaces, spell "**face**."

Measures (or Bars)

Notes on a staff are divided into **measures** (or "bars") to help you keep track of where you are in the song.

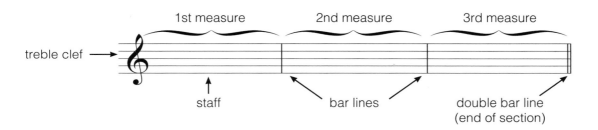

Time Signatures (or Meters)

A **time signature** (or "meter") indicates how many beats will appear in each measure. It contains two numbers: the top number tells you how many beats will be in each measure; the bottom number says what type of note will equal one beat.

☞ *R*elax for a while, read through it again later, and then move on.
(Trust us — as we go through the book, you'll start to understand it.)

LESSON 1
It's time to play something!

We're tuned. We're relaxed. We're comfortable. And we're eager to play. Let's get down to business...

As you know from page 4, the left hand "selects" a note by depressing a string at a fret, while the right hand "plays" that string with the pick. Playing an **open string** means playing a string without pressing a fret.

String 1: E

Forget 2-6, let's concentrate on string 1 for now. Use the photos and fingerboard diagrams to play your first notes.

Play string 1 open and you will hear E. This note is indicated on a treble clef staff like this:

E

Play string 1 while pressing fret 1 with finger 1 and you will hear F. This note is indicated on the staff like this:

F

Press fret 3 with finger 3 and play G. (You can leave finger 1 on fret 1, if you like.) You guessed it, the note on the staff looks like this:

G

☞ *"What happened to fret 2?"*
That note is F-sharp. We'll explain "sharps" later.

Put it to good use...

Three notes in about three minutes—not bad progress, huh? Practice these notes again and again using the following tunes. (If you need a review of rhythmic values or time signatures, turn back to pages 6 and 7.)

Just like reading a book, go to the next line in the song as soon as you reach the end of each staff. However, when you see this symbol (▤), you are at the end of that song.

Fingering Tip #1: When pressing a fret, use only the fingertip, so that other strings are not touched by the same finger.

Don't be afraid to repeat these tunes over and over, playing them a little bit faster each time. Then, when you're ready, we'll move on to Lesson 2.

LESSON 2

Moving on...

Welcome back! Now you know three notes and three songs. Okay, we admit they were boring ones, but let's learn three more notes and some better songs.

HELPFUL HINT: Take a few seconds, flip back to page 3 and make sure your guitar is still in tune.

String 2: B

We'll learn string 2 the same way we learned string 1 (yes, even skipping fret 2 again). The only difference is the new pitches you will hear:

Play string 2 open. That's B. This note lies on the middle line of the treble clef staff:

Play string 2 while pressing fret 1 with finger 1 and you get C, which lies on the space just above B:

Press fret 3 with finger 3 and you have D. It sits just above C:

Why not fret 2 again? This time fret 2 is C-sharp.
We'll introduce "sharps" in Lesson 3.

Put it to more good use...

Practice your new notes with this short exercise:

TRACK 5 B–C–D

Now here are some tunes (much better ones, we might add) to practice your six notes. Don't be embarassed to review E, F, and G again before playing.

Ode to Joyful Rock

TRACK 6

☞ **Fingering Tip #2:** When changing fingers from string 1 to string 2, try to let your eyes move ahead in the music and move the correct finger to the correct string before the next note occurs.

Blues for My Dog

TRACK 7

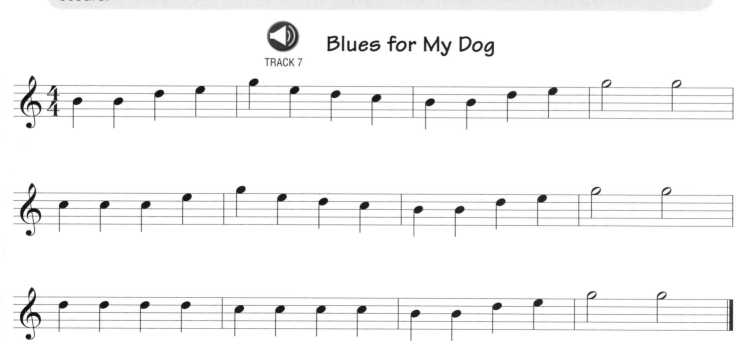

Remember to keep your fingers arched at all times (while playing, that is).

Rock to My Lou

TRACK 8

Rockin' the Bells

TRACK 9

Fingering Tip #3: When playing a higher note, leave the lower note depressed. For example, leave finger 1 on F while pressing finger 3 on G. When you go back to F, simply lift finger 3.

Give My Regards to Broadway

TRACK 10

If your fingertips hurt, take a break. But never fear—the more you practice, the faster they will toughen up.

SOME MORE NOTES ON MUSIC
(...pardon the pun!)

Before we go to Lesson 3, we want to tell you some more about the hieroglyphics of music.

Rests

A musical **rest** is a pause. Rests are like notes in that they have their own rhythmic values, instructing the musician how long (or how many beats) to pause:

whole rest	half rest	quarter rest
(four beats)	(two beats)	(one beat)

In the following 4/4 example, you will play E, E, pause, E, pause, pause, pause, pause, E, E, pause, pause, E, pause, pause, E:

Take a Load Off

TRACK 11

IMPORTANT: A rest does not mean rest your fingers or put down your guitar! During a rest, you should get your fingers into position for the next set of notes.

When the Saints Go Marching In

TRACK 12

LESSON 3

Moving on...

Unbelievable—six notes already. You're a fast learner! How 'bout another string? (Make sure you're still in tune, if not—page 3.)

String 3: G

String 3 is a bit different from strings 1 and 2. String 3 will get finger 2 into the action, and we'll skip fret 1 this time...

   Play string 3 open. That's G, which is written on the second line of the treble clef staff:

   Play string 3 while pressing fret 2 with finger 2 and you get A. This note lies on the space between G and B:

☞ **W**e realize that you already learned another G on string 1, but since the musical alphabet only has the letters A through G, this type of repetition will eventually occur with all note names.

Let's practice these two new notes. (WARNING: With only two notes, this exercise is rather boring. Hang in there...)

 Two-Note Jam

TRACK 13

Only after you're convinced you know these two notes, should you move on to the next page...

Yankee Doodle

TRACK 14

Remember to practice slowly. Speed up the **tempo** as you become more confident with the notes.

Red River Rock

TRACK 15

If you need, put the guitar down and just recite the note names of the song. Then practice locating the notes on the guitar before actually playing. Most importantly, just have fun!

Aura Lee

TRACK 16

☞ Take a break, When you return, review Lessons 1, 2, and 3.

Accidentals

Music is made up of **half steps** and **whole steps**. Each fret on your guitar equals one half step. When a song requires a note to be only a half step higher or lower, a symbol is placed by that note.

One half step higher is called a **sharp** and looks like a tic-tac-toe board: ♯

One half-step lower is called a **flat** and looks like a lower-case b: ♭

EXCEPTION TO THE RULE: From E to F is only a half step; from B to C is only a half step. (Look at the white keys on the piano diagram on page 3.)

Since you only got two notes in Lesson 3...

We'll give you not one but two more notes! And they're both sharps!! Return to strings 1 and 2 and check 'em out.

  On string 1, press fret 2 with finger 2 and hear your first sharp:

  On string 2, press fret 2 with finger 2 and you'll hear C-sharp:

Try this short exercise with your new "sharp-looking" notes:

 I Know Two Sharps

TRACK 17

Now you know why we skipped fret 2 earlier...
On string 1 (E), one fret higher than F is F-sharp.
On string 2 (B), one fret higher than C is C-sharp.

Rockin' Sharps

TRACK 18

This Old Man

TRACK 19

☞ A **natural sign** (♮) cancels an accidental on a note, returning it to its natural pitch.

Private Eye Groove

TRACK 20

☞ Watch the music, not your fingers!
(Your brain has enough going on—don't try to memorize the tunes, too!)

LESSON 4

A little bit lower now...

Let's check your progress: three strings and ten notes. It's like eating chips—just can't stop, can you? Well then, let's tackle another string...

String 4: D

Learning string 4 is like string 3 (we'll skip fret 1 again), but this time you get three notes:

  Playing string 4 open is D, written just below the staff:

  Fret 2, finger 2 is E, which occupies the first line of the staff:

  Press fret 3 with finger 3 to hear F:

 D–E–F

TRACK 21

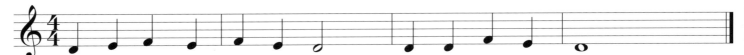

Now play the new D, E, and F followed by the old D, E, and F.

 Same Name, Different Note

TRACK 22

☞ **S**ound similar? The old D, E, and F sound one **octave** higher than the new ones. An octave means eight notes apart. You also know two more notes that are an octave apart. HINT: string 3 open and string 1, fret 3.

Enough of that...let's jam!

Play the following exercise with your new D, E, and F (the ones on string 4, that is):

DEF Jam
TRACK 23

Now a tune that switches between octaves:

Crosswalk Blues
TRACK 24

> ☞ FRIENDLY REMINDER: The next song is in 3/4 meter. That is, three beats (quarter notes) per measure. If you need a review, flip back to page 7.

House of the Rising Sun
TRACK 25

EIGHTH NOTES

Can you spare a quarter? How 'bout an eighth?

An **eighth note** has a flag on it:

Two eighth notes equal one quarter note (or one beat in 4/4 and 3/4). To make it easier on the eyes, eighth notes are connected with a **beam**:

To count eighth notes, divide the beat into two and use "and" between the beats:

Practice this by first counting out loud while tapping your foot on the beat, then play the notes while counting and tapping:

What about the rest?

Eighth rests are the same, but you...pause. Count, tap, play, and pause with the following:

Now try some songs that use eighth notes and rests. (Keep that foot going!)

Rockin' Riff

TRACK 26

Excellent. But don't stop there...

Pickups

Instead of starting a song with rests, a **pickup measure** can be used. A pickup measure simply deletes the rests. So, if a pickup has only one beat, you count "1, 2, 3" and start playing on beat 4:

Try these songs with pickup measures:

Snake Charmer

TRACK 27

Amazing Grace

TRACK 28

Fantastic! Play them again and again. Remember the three Ps: practice, patience and pace yourself.

More half steps...

Let's add two more notes: another F-sharp and B-flat.

On string 4, wake up finger 4 and place it on fret 4. There's your new F-sharp.

On string 3, press fret 3 with finger 3. This is B-flat, which appears on the staff like this:

Minuet

TRACK 29

☞ DON'T FORGET: A **natural** sign (♮) cancels an accidental on a note, returning it to its natural pitch.

Bach Rock

TRACK 30

22

Alouette

TRACK 31

> ☞ **Repeat signs** (𝄆 ⋮ ⋮ 𝄇) tell you to repeat everything in between. If only one sign appears (𝄇), repeat from the beginning of the piece.

Here are three more great examples for your riffing pleasure...

Hard Rock Riff

TRACK 32

Eastern Riff

TRACK 33

Hiphop Riff

TRACK 34

Now is a good time to check your tuning.

LESSON 5

Almost there...

Are you relaxed? Still in tune? Ready for another string?

String 5: A

Play string 5 open. This is A. (Can you play another A? HINT: string 3.) The new A is written on two leger lines:

A

Finger and play fret 2 on string 5 and you get B. (Can you play B an octave higher?) The new B is written under just one leger line:

B

Play fret 3 of string 5 and that's C. (Where's the other C you learned?) The new C is on the first leger line:

C

Practice your new A, B, and C (slowly, of course):

 A–B–C

TRACK 35

 Run, Don't Walk

TRACK 36

24

TIES & DOTS

Ties

A **tie** connects two notes and tells you to extend the first note to the end of the tied note:

1   2   3   (4   1)   (2)   3   (4   1   2)   3   4

Remember to always count out loud until you begin to think and feel the beat.

Dots

Another way to extend the value of a note is to use a **dot**. A dot extends the note by one-half of its value. Most common is the **dotted half** note:

$$\text{half note} \quad + \quad \text{dot} \quad = \quad \text{dotted half note}$$

half note   +   dot   =   dotted half note
(two beats)   (one beat)   (three beats)

You'll encounter dotted half notes in many songs, especially those that use 3/4 meter.

Greensleeves

TRACK 40

Watch for the ties and dots as we continue...

Scarborough Fair

And now, please rise (but only if you have a shoulder strap)...

Star-Spangled Banner

LESSON 6

Last, but definitely not least...

Did you think you'd never get to the last string? Well, it's here, you're ready, let's learn it...

String 6: E

The funny thing is: you already know this string! It's exactly like string 1 (except it's thicker and sounds two octaves lower). So, every note you learned on string 1, you know the same on string 6.

Just for kicks, play string 6 open. That's "low E." This new E (your third so far) lies just below the third leger line:

Press fret 1 with finger 1 and you hear "low F."

While still pressing F, press fret 3 with finger 3 and that's "low G."

 Sixth String Strut

TRACK 43

Octaves

Play your new E, F, and G, followed by your first E, F, and G (on string 1, that is)...

Now add the other set of E, F, and G (on strings 4 and 3)...

☞ HELPFUL HINT: Let your eyes read ahead of the note that you're actually playing.

Take Me Onto the Stage, Please

TRACK 44

Great! But since you know all six strings, there's just no stopping. Turn the page...

Pack Up Your Troubles

The next two songs have a **dotted quarter** note, which get one and one-half beats:

quarter note	+	dot	=	dotted quarter note
(1 beat)		(1/2 beat)		(1 1/2 beats)

Listen to the next audio track while you clap the beat. Can you feel the rhythm of the dotted quarter? Try playing it.

More Rock and Roll

Battle Hymn of Rock

TRACK 47

Oh, what the heck…here are two more notes for you (both played with finger 1)

One octave lower than the previous B-flat you learned:

Another first fret flat:

Minor Jam

TRACK 48

Terrific! Wanna learn to play chords? Turn the page…

LESSON 7

Fear of flying solo...

Congratulations! You know all six strings. This is a terrific time to tell you about two of guitarists' favorite things: **chords** and **tablature**.

What's a chord?

Chords consist of three or more notes played simultaneously. Listen to Track 49 for some examples of chords:

TRACK 49   G – Em – C – D7

Chords are good to know. For one thing, if you don't want to play a solo melody, you can simply play the chords of a song while you sing the melody.

Introducing Tablature or "TAB"

Since chords are tricky, we'll use a special type of music notation called **tablature**. It consists of six lines (the spaces don't count), one line for each string. The number written on the line indicates which fret to play on that string:

E	**A**	**B and E**
(string 4, fret2)	(string 5, open)	(strings 1 and 2, open, played together)

TRACK 50   **Tab This!**

Let's dive right in and learn three commonly used **major** chords.

3 cool chords

IMPORTANT: When playing a chord, strum only the strings that are part of the chord. **Xs** above the grid tell you to avoid strumming that string; **Os** indicate an **open string**. The dots are left-hand fingerings (fingering numbers are below).

Use a downstroke, starting with string 5 and hear your first chord:

Arch those fingers and strum all six strings for G:

Check your fingers. Are they arched? Also, be sure you only strum strings 4 through 1 for D:

☞ A **chord line** is written above the staff, indicating which chords to play.

Chord Practice

TRACK 51

Just like single notes, a chord has rhythmic value. For example, a half-note chord gets only one strum and lasts for two beats.

In most music, chords follow certain patterns called **chord progressions**. Here is a chord progression using G–D–C:

Unplugged

TRACK 52

The next song uses a common two-measure chord progression similar to many rock songs, including "Louie, Louie" and "Wild Thing."

Three-Chord Cliché

TRACK 53

FRIENDLY TIP: If your chord sounds bad, you probably muted or muffled a string or two. Check your fingers and play each string, one at a time, to find the "problem string(s)." Then readjust your finger(s).

Play the following songs by reading only from the chord line. Strum once for each beat (four strums per measure). Sing along with the melody...

Good Night, My Fans
TRACK 54

Good   night,   my   fans.   Good   night,   my   fans.

Good   night,   my   fans.   I'm   going   to   leave   you   now.

Worried Man Blues
TRACK 55

It   takes   a   wor - ried   man   to   sing   a   wor - ried

song.   It   takes   a   wor - ried   man   to   sing   a   wor - ried

song.   It   takes   a   wor - ried   man   to   sing   a   wor - ried

song.   I'm   wor - ried   now,   but   I   won't   be   wor - ried   long.

Now play them again and vary the number of times you strum for each chord. For example, you might want to strum along with every melody note, or just once for each chord (or maybe somewhere in the middle).

LESSON 8

It's the minor things that count...

Major chords weren't that tough, huh? How 'bout three **minor** chords?

Chords: Em, Am, and Dm

A **chord suffix** tells you what type of chord to play. Major chords have no suffix, only the letter name. But minor chords use the suffix "m" after the letter name.

Em

  Hey, this one's easy! Strum it twice:

Am

  The "low A" is the **root note** (lowest pitch) here, so be sure you avoid the sixth string when you strum:

Dm

  Only the top four strings this time (just like with D major). Keep those fingers arched:

Listen to these chords on the audio track and then play along...take your time.

More Chord Practice

TRACK 56

36

Chord Trax #1

Chord Trax #2

For the next example, try using an **upstrum** (↑) for the last eighth note in each measure. (That is, strum upwards starting with string 1).

Chord Trax #3

A minor question...

As you can see (and hear), a major chord is no bigger (or any more important) than a minor one, it's just a name. So what's the difference between them? Listen to them again...

QUICK AND EASY: Major chords sound "happy" and minor chords sound "sad."

Sing and use the chord line to strum along to the next two songs.

When Johnny Comes Rocking Home

TRACK 60

Scarborough Fair

TRACK 61

Are you go-ing to Scar-bor-ough Fair? Pars-ley sage, rose-ma-ry and thyme. Re-mem-ber me to one who lives there. ___ For once she was a true love of mine.

Sometimes, guitarists prefer to read chords from **slash notation**. (Who wouldn't?) Strum once for every time you see a " **/** " symbol. The second time through, follow the chord line and try variations of downstrokes and upstrokes.

Chord Trax #4

TRACK 62

Chord Trax #5

TRACK 63

LESSON 9

One last note...

All six strings, major chords, minor chords—you almost know everything! Here's a new one, though...

Note: High A

Go back to string 1 (E), wake up finger 4 and place it behind fret 5.

  As you can see, "high A" is written on the first leger line above the staff.

A

 Just for Practice

TRACK 64

Practice "high A" with the following two-octave exercise:

🔊 **A to A to A**

TRACK 65

Do you realize what you just played? That was your first musical **scale**—A minor. And a two-octave scale at that!

What's a musical scale?

Scales are arrangements of notes in specific (sequential) patterns. Most scales use eight notes with the top and bottom notes being an octave apart. The one you just played started on A and used a **minor pattern**, thus it was the A minor scale.

Practice "high A" lots more with these songs.

Danny Boy

TRACK 66

Oh, Dan - ny boy, the crowd is cheer - ing for _____ you. _____ Out in their

seats, they wait for you to play. _____ And when you play, you'll

hear them sing - ing with _____ you. You are the best. At least that's what they say.

Auld Lang Syne

TRACK 67

LESSON 10

You've got the power!

A great thing to know about (which a lot of beginning guitar books won't teach you) is **power chords**. These three power chords use the suffix "5."

Power Chords: E5, A5, D5

You will only play two strings at a time. **Mute** the higher ones by softly resting your right-hand palm on them.

E5

On fret 2 of strings 5 and 4, press with finger 1. Now play strings 6 and 5 only.

A5

Move finger 1 to fret 2 of string 4 and play strings 5 and 4.

D5

Move to string 3 and play strings 4 and 3.

 Move It!

TRACK 68

HELPFUL HINT: As you move your left hand down one string,
move your right hand down one string.

42

Go slowly, speed up the tempo each time you repeat, and remember to watch the music, not your fingers!

Power Chord Stomp

TRACK 69

Movin' and Rockin'

TRACK 70

CAUTION: You are nearing the end of this book.
Run to your local music dealer and get **FastTrack Guitar 2**!

LESSON 11

Time to charge admission...

This isn't really a Lesson...it's a jam session!

All the *FastTrack* books (guitar, keyboard, bass and drums) have the same last section. This way, you can either play by yourself along with the audio or form a band with your friends.

So, whether the band's on the audio tracks or in your garage, let the show begin...

TRACK 71
full
band

TRACK 72
minus
guitar

Exit for Freedom

Unplugged Ballad

TRACK 73
full band

TRACK 74
minus guitar

Billy B. Badd

TRACK 75
full
band

TRACK 76
minus
guitar

Conclusion

Bravo! Encore!!
Remember to practice often and always try to learn more about your instrument.

WAIT! DON'T GO YET!

Even though we hope (and expect) that you will review this entire book again and again, we thought you might like a "cheat sheet," referencing all the notes and chords you learned.

Notes in first position:

Chords in first position:

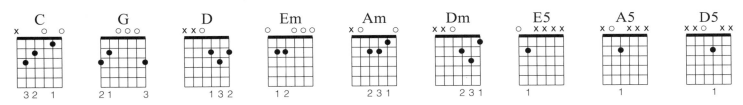

Where to go from here...

Finally, we'd like to suggest five things to help you continue to master the guitar:

1. **Repetition is the best way to learn.** Review the exercises in this book again and again until all the notes and chords are easily playable without even thinking about them.

2. **Buy "FastTrack Guitar: Book 2,"** which teaches many more notes, chords, techniques, and music fundamentals. Hopefully, you can find it at the same store that had this book.

3. **Buy "FastTrack Guitar: Chords and Scales,"** an excellent reference book with over 2,000 chords, as well as basic chord theory, scales, modes, and common chord progressions.

4. **Buy "FastTrack Guitar: Songbook 1,"** which includes classic songs from the Beatles, Clapton, Hendrix, Elton John, and more!

5. **Enjoy what you do.** Whether it's practicing, picking, jamming, performing, tuning, or even cleaning your guitar, do it with a smile on your face. Life's too short.

See you next time...

SONG INDEX

TRACK	SONG TITLE	PAGE	TRACK	SONG TITLE	PAGE
1	Tuning	3	39	Boogie Blues	25
2	E-F-G	9	40	Greensleeves	26
3	First Song	9	41	Scarborough Fair	27
4	Three-Note Rock	9	42	Star-Spangled Banner	27
5	B-C-D	11	43	Sixth String Strut	28
6	Ode to Joyful Rock	11	44	Take Me Onto the Stage, Please	29
7	Blues for My Dog	11	45	Pack Up Your Troubles	30
8	Rock to My Lou	12	46	More Rock and Roll	30
9	Rockin' the Bells	12	47	Battle Hymn of Rock	31
10	Give My Regards to Broadway	12	48	Minor Jam	31
11	Take a Load Off	13	49	Chord Examples	32
12	When the Saints Go Marching In	13	50	Tab This!	32
13	Two-Note Jam	14	51	Chord Practice	33
14	Yankee Doodle	15	52	Unplugged	34
15	Red River Rock	15	53	Three-Chord Cliché	34
16	Aura Lee	15	54	Good Night, My Fans	35
17	I Know Two Sharps	16	55	Worried Man Blues	35
18	Rockin' Sharps	17	56	More Chord Practice	36
19	This Old Man	17	57	Chord Trax #1	37
20	Private Eye Groove	17	58	Chord Trax #2	37
21	D-E-F	18	59	Chord Trax #3	37
22	Same Name, Different Note	18	60	When Johnny Comes Rocking Home	38
23	DEF Jam	19	61	Scarborough Fair	39
24	Crosswalk Blues	19	62	Chord Trax #4	39
25	House of the Rising Sun	19	63	Chord Trax #5	39
26	Rockin' Riff	20	64	Just for Practice	40
27	Snake Charmer	21	65	A to A to A	40
28	Amazing Grace	21	66	Danny Boy	41
29	Minuet	22	67	Auld Lang Syne	41
30	Bach Rock	22	68	Move It!	42
31	Alouette	23	69	Power Chord Stomp	43
32	Hard Rock Riff	23	70	Movin' and Rockin'	43
33	Eastern Riff	23	71	Exit for Freedom (full band)	44
34	Hiphop Riff	23	72	Exit for Freedom (minus guitar)	44
35	A–B–C	24	73	Unplugged Ballad (full band)	45
36	Run, Don't Walk	24	74	Unplugged Ballad (minus guitar)	45
37	British Invasion	25	75	Billy B. Badd (full band)	46
38	Drunken, Rockin' Sailor	25	76	Billy B. Badd (minus guitar)	46